SandCastle

Rhyming Riddles

Overdue
Kangaroo

Pam Scheunemann

Consulting Editor Monica Marx, M.A./Reading Specialist

ABDO
Publishing Company

Published by SandCastle™, an imprint of ABDO Publishing Company, 4940 Viking Drive, Edina, Minnesota 55435.

Printed in the United States.

Credits
Edited by: Pam Price
Curriculum Coordinator: Nancy Tuminelly
Cover and Interior Design and Production: Mighty Media
Photo Credits: Brand X Pictures, Comstock, Corbis Images, Eyewire Images, Hemera, PhotoDisc, Rubberball Productions, Stockbyte

Library of Congress Cataloging-in-Publication Data

Scheunemann, Pam, 1955-
    Overdue kangaroo / Pam Scheunemann.
      p. cm. -- (Rhyming riddles)
    Includes index.
    Summary: Illustrations and easy-to-read text present riddles with two-word, rhyming answers.
    ISBN 1-59197-462-3
    1. Riddles, Juvenile. [1. Riddles. 2. Jokes. 3. Reading.] I. Title.

PN6371.5.S357 2003
818'.602--dc21

2003048003

SandCastle™ books are created by a professional team of educators, reading specialists, and content developers around five essential components that include phonemic awareness, phonics, vocabulary, text comprehension, and fluency. All books are written, reviewed, and leveled for guided reading, early intervention reading, and Accelerated Reader® programs and designed for use in shared, guided, and independent reading and writing activities to support a balanced approach to literacy instruction.

Let Us Know

After reading the book, SandCastle would like you to tell us your stories about reading. What is your favorite page? Was there something hard that you needed help with? Share the ups and downs of learning to read. We want to hear from you! To get posted on the ABDO Publishing Company Web site, send us e-mail at:

sandcastle@abdopub.com

SandCastle Level: Beginning

Hinkety pinketies

are words that rhyme and each have three syllables.

Each riddle in this book has an answer that is a hinkety pinkety.

The answers are on page 22

What do you call a late marsupial?

See answer on page 22

Be there by 4:30!

5

What is another name for the White House?

See answer on page 22

What do you call a messy theft?

See answer on page 22

9

What is the
answer to
a trash
problem?

See answer on page 22

What do you call a free trip?

See answer on page 22

What do you call a kid who is a whiz at adding numbers?

See answer on page 22

2+5=7
10+3=13
8+7=15
9+2=11
14+6=20

15

What do you
call a raffle
of clay jars?

See answer on page 22

What do you
call a frozen
three-wheeler?

See answer on page 22

What do you call a fair investigator?

See answer on page 22

The Answers

Page 4
overdue kangaroo

Page 6
president's residence

Page 8
slobbery robbery

Page 10
pollution solution

Page 12
vacation donation

Page 14
addition magician

Page 16
pottery lottery

Page 18
icicle tricycle

Page 20
objective detective

Glossary

donation   a gift usually given to a fund or a cause

marsupial   animals that have pouches to carry their young

objective   making observations based upon the facts alone

overdue   late

residence   a dwelling in which somebody lives

solution   the answer to a problem

About SandCastle™

A professional team of educators, reading specialists, and content developers created the SandCastle™ series to support young readers as they develop reading skills and strategies and increase their general knowledge. The SandCastle™ series has four levels that correspond to early literacy development in young children. The levels are provided to help teachers and parents select the appropriate books for young readers.

Emerging Readers
(no flags)

Beginning Readers
(1 flag)

Transitional Readers
(2 flags)

Fluent Readers
(3 flags)

These levels are meant only as a guide. All levels are subject to change.

To see a complete list of SandCastle™ books and other nonfiction titles from ABDO Publishing Company, visit www.abdopub.com or contact us at:

4940 Viking Drive, Edina, Minnesota 55435 • 1-800-800-1312 • fax: 1-952-831-1632